Ital Food

EATING RASTAFARIAN STYLE

ANNEMARIE TROEDER

LMH PUBLISHING LIMITED

©2013 Annemarie Troeder
First Edition
Reprint 2018
10 9 8 7 6 5 4 3 2

Editors: Kenisha T. Duff and Kishanie Whyte
Cover Design: Sanya Dockery
Book Design, Layout & Typesetting: Sanya Dockery

Published by LMH Publishing Limited
Suite 10-11
Sagicor Industrial Park
7 Norman Road
Kingston C.S.O., Jamaica
Tel: 876-938-0005
Fax: 876-759-8752
Email: lmhbookpublishing@cwjamaica.com
Website: www.lmhpublishing.com

Printed in Canada   ISBN: 978-976-8202-68-0

NATIONAL LIBRARY OF JAMAICA CATALOGUING-IN-PUBLICATION DATA

Troeder, Annemarie
   Ital food : eating Rastafarian style ? Annemarie Troeder

   p. ; cm.
ISBN 978-976-8202-68-0 (pbk)

1. Cookery, Jamaican   2. Cookery, Tropical
3. Rastafarian movement

641.5679676 - dc 22

I would like to thank all the Rastafarians who helped to make this book possible.

Conversion Table

LIQUID MEASURES

1 cup	8 fluid ounces	½ pint	237 ml
2 cups	16 fluid ounces	1 pint	474 ml
4 cups	32 fluid ounces	1 quart	946 ml
2 pints	32 fluid ounces	1 quart	0.964 liters
4 quarts	128 fluid ounces	1 gallon	3.784 liters
8 quarts	one peck		
4 pecks	one bushel		
dash	less than ¼ teaspoon		

DRY MEASURES

3 teaspoons	1 tablespoon	½ ounce	14.3 grams	
2 tablespoons	⅛ cup	1 fluid ounce	28.3 grams	
4 tablspoons	¼ cup	2 fluid ounces	56.7 grams	
5⅓ tablespoons	⅓ cup	2.6 fluid ounces	75.6 grams	
8 tablespoons	½ cup	4 ounces	113.4 grams	1 stick butter
12 tablespoons	¾ cup	6 ounces	.375 pound	170 grams
32 tablespoons	2 cups	16 ounces	1 pound	453.6 grams
64 tablespoons	4 cups	32 ounces	2 pounds	907 grams

Table of Contents

Introduction

There is always a choice in what you eat. In this book, the second book in the 'Likkle' Jamaican Cookbook Series, you will learn about ital food. The approach is not academic, it's an exciting collection of delicious ital food recipes that are easy and fun to prepare.

A cookbook with a difference, the author has included some interesting personalities who were happy to share a few of their personal recipes and ways of preparing ital food.

What Is Ital Food?

Ital food is the type of food that the majority of practising Rastafarians eat. The word ital is derived from the English word 'vital', with the initial syllable replaced by I. Rastafarians do this to many words to signify the unity of the speaker with all of nature.

There are a few universal rules to ital living, but the most important of them is to adhere to an ital diet. This is done to increase 'Livity', which is the life essence that Rastafarians generally believe resides in all of us, given to us by the Almighty.

A common tenet of Rastafarian belief is the sharing of a central Livity among living things, and what is put into one's body should enhance Livity rather than reduce it. The general principle is that food should be natural, pure and from the earth. Rastafarians therefore tend to avoid food that is chemically modified or contains artificial additives such as preservatives and flavourings. Many also avoid adding salt to food, especially salt with iodine.

Most Rastafarians do not eat pork and shellfish as they are considered to be scavengers, and some avoid the consumption of red meat. There are also those who do not eat fish over twelve inches in length and some are strict vegetarians or vegans. Under the strictest interpretation of ital, food that is preserved by canning or drying, or even prepared in metal utensils are avoided. In this instance, only wooden and clay cooking pots are used. Not all Rastafarians follow the strictest interpretation.

Perhaps the most popular ital dish is the Ital Stew, also known as Veggie Stew. It consists of ingredients such as red peas, onion, garlic, sweet potato, pimento grains, coconut milk and scotch bonnet peppers.

One of the amazing ways of preparing food the ital way is by using the sun. One of the proponents of this method of cooking is Dr. Aris LaTham, one of the world's top vegetarian chefs. He operates the Sunfire Natural Life Institute at Coyaba River Garden in Ocho Rios.

Rastafarianism

Rastafarianism, or the Rastafari movement, is a religion and philosophy that accepts Haile Selassie I, the former Emperor of Ethiopia, as God incarnate, whom they call Jah. He is also seen as the Messiah, a part of the Holy Trinity, who the Bible promised us will return. The name Rastafari comes from Ras Tafari Makonnen, the pre-coronation name of Haile Selassie I.

The original Rastafarians drew their inspiration from the philosophies of Marcus Mosiah Garvey, who tried to unite black people with their rightful homeland, Africa. Garvey told black people to "look to Africa for the crowning of a king to know that your redemption is near". In 1930, Prince Ras Tafari Makonnen was crowned the new Emperor of Ethiopia. Upon his coronation, he claimed for himself the title of Emperor Haile Selassie I. This announcement was a monumental event that many blacks in Africa and the Americas saw as the fulfillment of Garvey's prophecy. After the crowning of Selassie, the Rastafari movement gained a following and officially began. A Jamaican, Leonard Howell, is widely credited as the founder of the religion.

Rastafarianism is an acephalous movement. With no clearly defined leader, the religion consists of groups, quasi-groups, and individuals who remain independent in spite of sharing the core beliefs. With the exception of two highly organized sects, the Bobos and the Twelve Tribes of Israel, most Rastafarians do not belong to a formal organization.

The practising of the Rastafarian faith is not as structured as most of the other world religions. The majority of worship occurs during rituals. There are two types of Rastafarian religious rituals. A Reasoning is a simple event where the Rastafarians gather and smoke marijuana; and discuss ethical, social and religious issues. The person who is given the honour to light the chillum also says a short prayer beforehand. A Binghi or Grounation is a holy day; the name Binghi is derived from Nyabinghi, believed to be an ancient, and now extinct, order of militant blacks in Eastern Africa that vowed to end oppression. Binghis are marked by much dancing, singing, feasting and the smoking of marijuana, and can last for several days.

The wearing of dreadlocks is very closely associated with the movement, though not universal among, or exclusive to its adherents. Rastafarians believe that dreadlocks are supported by the Bible. This support can be found in Leviticus 21:5, which states, "They shall not make baldness upon their head, neither shall they shave off the corner of their beard, nor make any cuttings in the flesh".

One of the most prominent symbols among Rastafarians is the lion. The lion represents Haile Selassie I, the Conquering Lion of Judah. Dreadlocks also symbolize the Lion of Judah (its mane) and rebellion against Babylon (modern society). For many Rastafarians, smoking marijuana or ganja as it is commonly called, is a spiritual act, often accompanied by Bible study. They consider it a sacrament that cleanses the body and mind, exalts the consciousness, facilitates peacefulness, and brings them closer to Jah. They believe that the smoking of marijuana enjoys Biblical sanction and is an aid to meditation and religious observance.

Rastafarians account for roughly ten percent of the Jamaican populace and has a little over a million followers worldwide. One of its most famous proponents was the late great reggae superstar, Bob Marley.

Recipes

BY ANNEMARIE TROEDER

Cabbage Rolls With Tofu Filling

INGREDIENTS:

2 onions	1 hot pepper
1 pack Tofu (1lb. 455 grams)	½ cup coconut oil
Cabbage with big leaves	1 whole wheat dinner roll
1 sweet pepper	1 tomato
2 cloves garlic	Trussing string
1 roasted breadfruit	1 plantain

METHOD:

*   Wash sweet pepper, tomato and hot pepper. Strip onions and garlic then wash. Separate cabbage leaves and wash with warm water.
*   Break whole wheat dinner roll into small pieces.
*   Dice sweet pepper, tomato, 1 onion, ½ hot pepper (remove seeds), garlic and combine with mashed tofu.
*   Combine diced ingredients and whole wheat dinner roll with tofu. Form into a roll.
*   Place roll on three cabbage leaves, starting with the smallest to the largest. Tie with trussing string.
*   Fry remaining onion and hot pepper in coconut oil. Add cabbage rolls and fry until golden brown.
*   Remove the string from the cabbage rolls before serving.

SIDE DISHES

Roast Breadfruit (usually roasted over an open fire) and Plantain

*   If you do not have an open fire, place breadfruit in a preheated oven at 350°F for about an hour until the skin is brown.
*   Wait until breadfruit is cool. Cut into slices and remove skin and core.
*   Peel plantain and slice into preferred shapes.
*   Fry plantain.
*   Fry breadfruit.

Whole Wheat Pizza

PIZZA BASE - INGREDIENTS

20 grams instant yeast

2 tablespoons vegetable oil

400 grams whole wheat flour

½ teaspoon sugar

1 ¼ cups water

METHOD:

- Preheat oven to about 180°C or 350°F.
- Sprinkle 20 grams of instant yeast into a medium bowl with ½ teaspoon of sugar and 1 ¼ cups of water.
- Add 2 tablespoons of vegetable oil.
- Add whole wheat flour and stir until blended.
- Cut into four pieces and form into balls.
- Leave the balls for about half an hour on a clean surface and cover with a cloth.
- Use a rolling pin to form the dough into 9 inch circles or measuring 20 cm in diameter.
- Put some tomato sauce on the pizza base.
- Bake for 15 - 20 minutes.

TO MAKE TOMATO SAUCE - INGREDIENTS:

1 kg peeled and boiled tomatoes

15 pimento seeds, 6 cloves

2 tablespoons brown sugar

Escallion and thyme (to taste)

2 onions

4 tablespoons vinegar

Oregano, Bay leaf

1 teaspoon coconut oil

METHOD:

- Chop the escallion and the onions with the tomatoes.
- Heat coconut oil in a pot and add everything except the sugar and the vinegar. Sauté.
- Drain the mixture through a sieve and add sugar and vinegar.
- Simmer until thick, cool down and refrigerate.

TOPPINGS:

Diced pineapples, sliced ripe bananas and shredded veggie cheese.

How to make the different toppings

ACKEE AND VEGGIE CHEESE

½ doz. ackees   1 tomato, diced

1 hot pepper (remove seeds), diced   1 onion, chopped

2 tablespoons coconut oil

Pick the ackee and remove the pinkish tissue. Wash and boil for no longer than 10 minutes. Heat chopped onion, diced tomato and diced hot pepper in coconut oil and then add the ackee. Mix carefully. Cook for 5 minutes.

CALLALOO AND VEGGIE CHEESE

A bundle of callaloo   2 tomatoes, diced

1 hot pepper (as desired)   1 onion, chopped

Milk from 1 small coconut   2 tablespoons coconut oil

Basil, thyme (to taste)

- Strip the callaloo, wash and cut very fine. Heat chopped onion, diced tomatoes and hot pepper in coconut oil.
- Add the callaloo and sauté for five minutes.
- Add callaloo topping to pizza base.
- Bake for 350° - 400°F or 200° - 220°C for 15 minutes.
- Sprinkle some fresh basil and/or thyme on top.

FURTHER TOPPINGS (AS EXAMPLES):
- Roasted fresh champignons (baby mushrooms) with parsley and ½ cup grated veggie cheese.
- Sliced tomatoes and onions.
- When you bake the base do so for only 5 minutes. Allow to cool, then pack them in appropriate bags and store them in a freezer. Remove from the freezer when needed. Heat the oven, put your toppings on and bake for 15 minutes.

Tofu with Walnuts & Mango Rice, served with String Beans

INGREDIENTS:

250 grams brown rice	1 mango
Milk from 1 small coconut	1 pack tofu
5 tablespoons coconut oil	250 grams walnuts
String beans	Tomato (to garnish)

Basil, oregano, thyme, escallion, garlic, cinnamon (to taste)

METHOD:
- Soak the slices of tofu in soya sauce overnight.
- Remove the coconut from husk. Wash and cut into small pieces. Blend with one cup of water. Pour contents from blender into cheese cloth or strainer to extract coconut milk.
- Cut walnuts very fine using a coffee mill or blender. Roll the tofu in the walnut mixture. Heat 4 tablespoons of coconut oil and fry until brown.
- Add coconut milk to 1½ cups of water. Bring to a boil. Add 250 grams brown rice. Simmer for 25 minutes. Add diced mangoes and cook for another 2 minutes. Sprinkle cinnamon on top.
- Boil the string beans for 10 minutes, heat 1 tablespoon of coconut oil and put the beans in for 1 minute.
- Serve with tomato slices.

Stuffed Mushrooms with Fried Breadfruit

INGREDIENTS:

2 lbs. champignons (mushrooms)

Escallion (to taste)

1 potato

1 hot pepper

1 cucumber

½ cup coconut oil

1 roasted breadfruit

1 stalk thyme

1 carrot

2 tomatoes

Parsley

Salt, to taste

METHOD:
- Wash mushrooms and remove stems.
- Boil mushrooms with escallion, thyme, potato, carrot and hot pepper (without seeds) for 10 minutes.
- Remove mushrooms, carrot, escallion, thyme and hot pepper from boiling water.
- Crush the carrot, escallion, thyme and add pepper to taste. Fill mushrooms with the mixture.
- Peel roasted breadfruit and then slice thinly.
- Heat ½ cup coconut oil in a medium-sized frying pan.
- Fry breadfruit until golden brown.
- Serve mushrooms with the fried breadfruit.
- Use tomatoes, cucumber and parsley to garnish.

Baked Fish Stuffed with Callaloo served with Bammy & Okra

INGREDIENTS:

1 fish	1 bundle callaloo
1 tomato, diced	1 onion, diced
1 hot pepper	1 dozen okra
8 tablespoons coconut oil	2 bammies
Black pepper (to taste)	Sea salt (optional)
2 cups coconut milk	

METHOD:
- Choose a medium to large sized fish, so that the filling can hold.
- Scale and clean the fish properly. Sprinkle black pepper on the fish.
- Soak bammies for 5 minutes in 1 cup coconut milk. If the bammies are frozen, leave to soak until they defrost.
- Fry bammies in 6 tablespoons of coconut oil.
- Wash and cut callaloo. Wash and slice okras.
- Fry diced tomato, onion and ½ of a hot pepper (without seeds) for 1 minute in 2 tablespoons of coconut oil. Remove half and mix it with callaloo. Steam callaloo for 10 minutes. Use the other half to mix with 1 cup of coconut milk. Add okra and boil until cooked.
- Stuff fish with callaloo. Pour coconut milk on top. Wrap in banana leaf and tie with a palm leaf. Bake fish at 350°F or 200°C or on a grill for 30 minutes.
- Serve with bammies and okra.

Pumpkin filled with Fish & Vegetables

This dish is ideal for using leftovers to fill the pumpkin.
You must see to it that the vegetables for the filling have
enough taste as you do not use salt.

INGREDIENTS:

A whole pumpkin	½ lb. carrot, diced
1 lb. small fish fillets, cubed	½ cup lime juice
1 large tomato, diced	1 large onion, diced
1 hot pepper	3 sticks celery
½ lb. diced broccoli	½ lb. corn
Escallion and thyme (to taste)	½ lb. diced zucchini
3 or 4 cloves garlic, diced	5 tablespoons coconut oil

METHOD:

- Soak fish fillets in ½ cup of lime juice for 15 minutes.
- Cut the top of the pumpkin and clean the inside. Save the seeds.
- Put the carrots, celery and the pumpkin (including the top) in the water and boil for 15 minutes. In the meantime, heat 4 tablespoons of coconut oil with diced garlic and add the cubed fish fillets. Cook the fish for five minutes.
- Remove pumpkin and other vegetables from the boiling water. Place pumpkin on baking sheet. Save the top.
- Heat 1 tablespoon of coconut oil.
- Sauté the boiled vegetables with broccoli, zucchini, diced onion, diced tomatoes, escallion, thyme and corn for 3 minutes.
- Fill the pumpkin and close with the top. Put the pumpkin seeds on the baking sheet (optional) and bake all in the oven at 350°F or 220°C for 40 minutes.
- To serve, cut the pumpkin into slices. Sprinkle with some of the roasted seeds. Serve with some rice if desired.

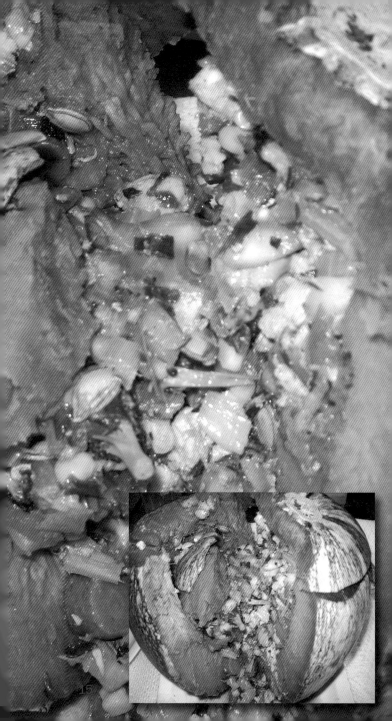

Whole Wheat Noodles & Tomato Sauce

Whole wheat noodles are sold at the supermarket.

INGREDIENTS:

Tomatoes (2 lbs/ 1 kg for 4 persons)	1 onion
1 garlic clove, finely chopped	½ cup escallion
½ teaspoon fresh oregano	1 cho cho
Raw cashew nuts (100 g per person)	2 tablespoons coconut oil
½ hot pepper without seeds	

METHOD:

- Boil the noodles (see package).
- Heat 2 tablespoons coconut oil and fry the chopped garlic.
- Put the vegetables and half of the oregano in a blender to cut.
- Steam the chopped vegetables with fried garlic for 10 minutes. Do not add water.
- Add the remaining oregano (leave a little to garnish) and serve over the noodles.
- Sprinkle some cashew nuts over it. Roasted nuts can also be used.

Fish Fritters with Grain & Papaya

FRITTERS – INGREDIENTS

Any kind of fish (¼ lb. for two fritters)　½ tomato

½ hot pepper (without seeds)　4 tablespoons coconut oil

3 slices whole wheat bread　½ onion

½ garlic

METHOD:
- Mix all in a blender, heat 3 tablespoons of coconut oil in a pan, form fritters and fry.

GRAIN - INGREDIENTS:

8 pimento seeds　2 cloves

¼ lb. whole DNS Grain (per person)

METHOD:
- Soak the grain in water overnight. Boil whole grain with pimento and cloves for one hour.

PAPAYA - INGREDIENTS:

1 large green papaya　½ hot pepper

1 tablespoon coconut oil　1 onion

Some papaya wine (or any red or rose)　½ sprig of thyme

METHOD:
- Wash and peel the papaya, take the seeds out and cut in cubes.
- Heat 1 tablespoon of coconut oil.
- Chop the onion, hot pepper (remove seeds) and thyme. Sauté for a minute then add the papaya cubes for an additional minute.
- Pour ½ cup of papaya wine over the papaya and leave for 10 minutes to cook then serve.

Fish Fillets with Pink Puree

FISH FILLETS - INGREDIENTS:

½ tablespoon Indian curry powder

1 small onion

Lemon juice

Black pepper (to taste)

Fish fillets

¼ lb. corn meal

6 tablespoons coconut oil

METHOD:

- Wash the fish fillets with lemon juice.
- Mix curry and cornmeal together.
- Put diced onions on the fish and sprinkle some black pepper over it.
- Coat the fish with the curry and cornmeal mixture.
- Heat the coconut oil and fry fish until golden brown.

PINK PUREE - INGREDIENTS:

2 lbs. Irish potatoes or yam

1 onion

2 tablespoons lemon juice

2 lbs. carrots

4 tablespoons coconut oil

1 plantain, sliced

METHOD:

- Peel the potatoes and the carrots, wash then boil. Leave some carrots raw for garnish.
- Cut the onion in rings, heat 4 tablespoons of coconut oil, fry golden and put aside.
- Fry plantain slices.
- Mash potatoes and carrots together.
- Serve the puree with the fried onion rings on top, shred the raw carrots over the fish. Put fried plantains on the side and sprinkle some lemon juice over the fish and the raw carrots.

Whole Wheat Apple Cake

INGREDIENTS:

225 grams oats	115 ml molasses
80 grams coconut, shredded	120 ml honey
160 grams walnuts, chopped	160 grams raisin
3 apples, shredded	160 grams apple juice
140 grams whole wheat flour	65 grams bran
2 tablespoons baking powder	12 half walnuts

METHOD:

- Soak the ingredients above (except flour, bran and baking powder) in apple juice for half an hour.
- Mix the flour with the baking powder and the bran, and add it to the ingredients being soaked in apple juice.
- Stir the mixture then pour into a baking tray. Put the 12 half walnuts on top. Bake for about 50-60 minutes at 180°C.

You can vary by using any other nut of your choice.

Duckunoo

(traditional changed to ital)

INGREDIENTS:

600 grams sweet potato, shredded

1 small dry coconut, shredded

1 tablespoon nutmeg

400 ml coconut milk

150 grams raisin

2 tablespoons vanilla

120 grams coconut oil

100 grams cornmeal

METHOD:

- Remove the coconut from the husk and the skin from the sweet potato and wash before shredding.
- Mix everything together to a smooth dough.
- Bring water to boil in a medium-sized sauté pot.
- Put 2 tablespoons of the dough in each banana leaf, fold and bind to a parcel.
- Put the parcel into the boiling water. Cook for 1 hour.

Recipes

&

Favourite Dishes

from some
INTERESTING PERSONALITIES

EMANUEL JOHNSON

Heading from Annotto Bay in the direction of Buff Bay, there is a small restaurant on the seaside with a lovely view of the sea.

Irie offers fish and chicken with vegetable rice and dumplings for ital and non-ital eaters.

As Emanuel's restaurant is situated at the seaside, he gets fresh fish daily from the fishermen.

He has been running his human service station for more than 25 years.

His favourite dish is fish with rice and peas.

CLIFTON JACKSON

Clifton Jackson is the proprietor of a garage in Spanish Town. The U-shaped complex where the garage is located also houses a restaurant, a multifunctional room, a library and a recording studio. Clifton organized, along with popular poet Mutabaruka, a mobile movie theatre (installed on a pick-up truck), which is sponsored by Jamaica's only all-reggae radio station, Irie FM. He travels around the island showing cultural and uplifting movies to the youth.

Pepperpot Soup (4 servings)

Bring 6 quarts of water to boil. Add two pounds of baddo (fold leaves) cut in fine pieces and allow to simmer for about 25 minutes. Add dasheen, coco and yam, and season with onions, 4-5 hot peppers, thyme and escallion, some pimento and susumber. Let it boil for 45 minutes.

MS. MINOTT

Ms. Minott took a term of experience as a teacher at Marjam Prep school in Ocho Rios before she finishes her studies at a university in Germany. She plans to make Jamaica her home one day.

Sip

- Bring some water to boil and add carrots, potatoes, dumplings, tomatoes, pumpkin, peas and cucumber.
- Season with thyme, escallion and garlic.
- Simmer for half an hour. It should be thicker than soup.

CLIFTON JOHNSON

"Cliff" Johnson has been running a music shop in the old market in Ocho Rios since 1988.

Ital Stew

- Bring water to boil and add peas, beans and coconut juice, escallion, thyme, pepper, carrots, turnips and dumplings.
- Allow to simmer, then add grated coconut, Irish potatoes, green bananas, yam, pumpkin and a little water.
- Simmer until thick.

JAH BLACKS (RUBIN)

   Jah Blacks runs a shop at 3 Miles, where he sells roots wine.
   He likes callaloo, cabbage, okra, pumpkin, different types of peas cooked in coconut water (veggie mix) and also peanut porridge.

RAS MABRAK

Ras Mabrak is a manufacturer of leather shoes, goat skin drums, decorative Rastafarian pencils and calabash bags.

His special recipe is ackee with okra, tomatoes, onions, pepper, peas and beans cooked in coconut milk.

ELISE KELLY

Elise Kelly has been at Irie FM since 1991. Her Reggae show "Easy Skanking" from 10 a.m. to 2 p.m. Monday to Thursday, is very interesting with good music and critical artiste interviews. She is often an MC at Reggae shows or festivals like 'Rebel Salute'.

She likes to cook and eat green gungo peas with rice and coconut milk, ackee run down with baked plantain and soursop juice with a little nutmeg and sugar (no lime, no milk), served with corn muffins or corn bread.

CURVIN MERCHANT (PAPA CURVIN)

Papa Curvin learnt music at the Alpha Boys School in Kingston. By the age of 18, he was one of the most famous drummers in Jamaica. With the band "Bamboos of Jamaica" formed in 1965, he toured on cruise ships with the German Quizmaster Peter Frankenfeld. He was the drummer of the backing band, Boney M. He played at hundreds of concerts from the early eighties in Germany. On the German Reggae scene he is known as "Germany's Grandfather of Roots Rock Reggae". He created the "REGGAE CENTER" in Hamburg for young musicians.

Tofu in Coconut Milk

INGREDIENTS:

Coconut milk

Garlic, onion

A big piece of tofu, diced

Thyme, escallion

Bird pepper

Brown rice

METHOD:

- Fry thyme, escallion, bird pepper, garlic and diced onion in coconut oil and add coconut milk. Simmer for half an hour, add tofu and cover for 5 minutes.
- Serve with brown rice and garnish with tomato, cucumber and okra.

GLENNVILLE GRAHAM

Mr. Graham is an art teacher at the MarJam Prep school in Ocho Rios and he runs an art gallery that is located close to Fern Gully.

He loves ackee cooked with just about any vegetable.

DR. ARIS LATHAM, PHD.

Dr. LaTham (born in Panama) started his food creations in 1979 with his sunfired foods company in New York City. He trained thousands of food chefs and created countless recipes. He taught Spanish, Swahili and English in the USA and Tanzania. He has been a vegetarian for over 35 years and living "raw" for the last 29 years. His sunfired gourmet food is famous all over the world, as well as his paradise pies.

You can attend his fasting and body detoxify programs at his Sunfire Natural Life Institute at Coyaba River Garden in Ocho Rios.

PROF-I (BARRINGTON REYNOLD)

Prof-I has been living "raw" for 32 years. He lives in Great Pond. When he and his family are doing their Nyabinghi ceremonies, I like to listen to them from home because it's close by.

He uses the sun to cook. Here are three recipes:

Mixed Vegatable

- Slice carrots and cho cho, cut string beans and pak choi.
- Put all in one pot with a little coconut oil. Stir until half cooked.

Do not over cook.

Ethiopean Stew

- First make coconut custard: blend dry coconut and then put to boil.
- Peel and dice Irish potatoes and add curry, onion, tomato, garlic, thyme and escallion. Place in oven.
- Remove from the oven when half-cooked and add the custard.

Ackee Butter

- Blend ½ of an onion, 3 tomatoes, 2 pieces of garlic, escallion and thyme. Put in the ackee, add sea salt and pepper if needed.

MUTABARUKA

Mutabaruka, born Alan Hope, is Jamaica's premier reggae poet. His first book of poetry, entitled "Outcry", (also the name of one of his music albums) was published in 1973. He promoted himself by doing readings at schools and the Kingston Creative Arts Centre. He has written several books and he also "wrote" a chapter of Jamaica's musical history with his exceptional music albums. You can listen to his radio show "Cutting Edge" on Irie FM from 10 p.m. to 2 a.m. direct or on the internet at www.iriefm.net.

No Fire Cooked Vegetable Dish

INGREDIENTS:

½ dozen ackees   Bundle of pak choi

A hand full of raisins   Clove of garlic

½ teaspoon of cayenne pepper   Basil leaf (optional)

4-6 tablespoons of virgin olive oil

METHOD:
- Wash pak choi and chop as small as possible and place in a bowl.
- Pick ackee and wash, making sure it is cleaned properly.
- Dice the ackee in tiny pieces. Place in the bowl. Add raisins, chopped garlic, pepper and basil leaf. Using a large spoon to stir contents, add Bragg Liquid Amino. Do not add salt.
- Stir again until vegetable starts to spring water.
- Pour olive oil in the bowl and stir.
- Serve with couscous or a vegetable salad.
- You can vary this recipe by adding sweet corn off the cob, or a dash of raw sunflower seeds and/or crushed Nori sheets*.

*   Nori is dried roasted seaweed. It will be processed to sheets 18-20 cm and 3 grams weight.

It is a source of iron, calcium, vitamin A, B, C1, iodine, protein (1/5 of milk (100ml), 1/5 of an egg), fiber (31.2mg/100g), and carotene.

Also in the 'Likkle' Jamaican Cookbook Series:

- Jamaican Jams, Marmalades & Jellies